My Father's Philosophy

Christina Richter

Copyright © 2019

All rights reserved. This book or any portion thereof may not be reproduced or used in any manner whatsoever without the express written permission of the author except for the use of brief quotations in a book review.

Printed in Australia
First Printing, 2019
ISBN: 978-0-6484641-2-9

White Light Publishing House
Melton, VIC, Australia 3337
whitelightpublishing.com.au

Other titles by Christina:

Learn to Self Heal

To PapaSun, my Dad. Thank you for being exactly what I needed to understand myself.

R.I.P. Love you in all ways

-Your daughter, Christina.

My Story

Have you ever had a 'Eureka' moment? Well I have. I remember it clearly as if it was yesterday.

I was relaxing in my warm scented bath when the proverbial brick hit. I was reflecting on why I had so many dysfunctional relationships with men. I was 34 years old and still making the same mistakes. Well, talk about connecting to the universe, the answer was clear and obvious.

I realised, for me to have happy functional relationships with men, I needed to have a happy functional relationship with my own father. My relationship with my father was nowhere near functional or happy. So, I remained in my warm bath, tuned into my feelings and mulled over this new piece of insight.

I concluded I had no way out. I wanted to attract men that did not lie, cheat or abuse me. For the sake of my growth I knew I needed to face my fear and confront my father. I knew by doing this my actions had the potential to divide my family. It was in my nature to always consider other people and what they thought of me, thereby neglecting myself.

Not this time. For once in my life, I would honour myself and put my needs first. After all, it was about my own growth and I was the only one who could direct it. With the decision made I spurred into action with a plan. I started reading self-help books on positive progress and toxic parents. I wrote a mission statement around my intention, what I expected and what I did not expect from my father. This process took me six months.

Meanwhile, I took a firm stand with my current partner at the time and told him I needed to do this without any interference from him. That was tough as my partner was a control freak and the relationship was, you guessed it, dysfunctional. Needless to say, he did not like that one bit.

I decided to call my dad which was my first call in seventeen years. I asked him to come to Sydney for a two-week holiday and to my genuine surprise, he agreed. I expected him to say no.

I can still remember the scene, the night he kicked me out into the rain.

His angry words were still etched in my memory. It was hard to forget my own father saying, "Don't come back. This is not your family".

"Never call the kids." That remark hurt the most. As the eldest, I felt close to my younger siblings due to helping raise them.

"Do not call our relatives to help you out. You are on your own now."

Even though I felt hurt and was devasted, I looked my father in the eye and vowed that I would not ask for any help from the relatives. I thought that even if it killed me, I would never give him that satisfaction. Although I was wet and cold in the night waiting for my taxi to arrive, I was not scared. I felt free. Free from the massive family responsibility I had and free from being scared all the time. I was relieved. I was seventeen years old.

I was born to German parents who loved me and three years later that was ripped apart due to my parents getting a divorce. At age four, my father remarried a Polynesian woman and I was introduced to a culture foreign to my own.

This was challenging for me as a sensitive child. As an adult, I realised this was an agreement I had made as part of my soul's integration and growth. Part of this soul agreement was to experience the ritual and discipline of the Catholic faith which my step-mother introduced, versus a philosophy of living that my father provided.

I can remember a time when Jehovah Witness came to the door spreading the word. Dad opened the door and when asked if he would like to know more about God he replied he was Catholic. When the Mormons came with their bible he replied he was Lutheran (which in fact he was).

It made no difference to my dad as he believed there was one power and it was for everyone. No one person or religion had a monopoly on God. Due to his example, this is the belief I hold and practice today.

My journey with my dad was not an easy one. He was a detached person and not very good at displaying affection or saying what he really meant. He would often lose his temper in the early years due to his frustration with life.

My father was born and raised during the second world war in Leipzig Germany and survival was part of his everyday life. He would tell us stories (later in life) about the bombs dropping so close to his house that the ground would shake.

Buchenwald concentration camp was a two-hour train ride from his home town. He would say that there was white stuff that floated down from the sky whenever he and his twin brother would go out and collect wood for the family home. He thought it was snow, except it wasn't cold. Understanding what I now know about energy, this must have been a dark... negative experience for his whole family.

He left school at fourteen years of age to go out into the world and forge his own path which he did successfully. During this time, he came to New Zealand, married and divorced my mother.

Being a sensitive and emotional child, I pined for my own mother and not understanding why at times, I was fearful of my father. It wasn't until I was in my mid-thirties that I started to examine my own beliefs. During that process I came to understand why I had my experiences as a child.

Growing up, I experienced the concept of God from two different points of view through my parents. I needed this to help me establish my own beliefs and path. Now an adult, I freely chose the path of Spiritualty and once I did that, my whole life started to change and develop in that area.

My father was a huge catalyst for my growth by purely being himself and living simply. I often would refer to him as Buddha as my father was abundant in heart as well as stature.

After my father and I made our peace with each other, I started to call more often and had regular visits. We went travelling together and we visited his home town. He would tell me stories of his life. He would often make short statements based on his wisdoms of life. This became a regular theme.

This book is a tribute to my father and what I have learnt from him.

How to use this Book

As spiritual beings in a physical body, we choose our life before birth. This includes our parents, family and all people that have a significant role to play in our growth.

Our journey with our chosen parents is usually uncomfortable; that is because we are here on the planet to learn and grow into ourselves.

My Fathers Fhilosophy is like a tarot deck. Simple instructions set below,

- Clear your mind
- Set your intention
- Ask your question
- Open to any page to receive a guided quote

Remember, read the message within the message and ask yourself, "how does this relate to me?"

For example, the message may be, "My greatest achievement has been my kids". Then, look at the achievements in your life or what is it you really wish to achieve and do it.

Blessings to you all.

Eat well. Have a garden so you know what you put into your body.

If it comes from your garden, you know it's good for you.

No point complaining. No one listens to you anyway.

My greatest achievement has been my kids.

If you don't ask, you don't get.

Work for what you want.

Help others only if you can afford to.

Live simply, pay your bills.

Cook with love. Eat with appetite.

Accept all people as they are and if they are not good for you, then step away.

Nothing is for free, except for the warm sun on your face.

It doesn't cost much to make people happy.

Smile and laugh more, it costs nothing.

If you have a win in life, share the gift.

Just be happy, life is short.

If you make a mistake in life, it's your mistake.

Be sure about your partner in life
because you have to live with them.
Don't complain about it later.

No matter who you are or what you have done, God knows the truth.

Don't worry, be happy…

You're number one.

Laugh a lot as it is healthy.

Heal all wounds as anger will only make you sick.

Go with life rather than against it,
you will be happier.

Always see the best in others until they show you otherwise.

Achieve something worth leaving behind.

Do not appear to be a good person,
be a good person.

You can fool yourself and others, but the man upstairs will always know.

Have no regrets, you will pass on easier.

I have friends from the United Kingdom, Holland, and Italy and we all get along. Why can't the rest of the world? What is their problem?

Make the best of what you have got.

Happiness is sharing a beer with friends.

Things happen in life. Holding onto the past only holds you back.

Better to give if you can. This act makes you happier and you feel better. Also, it will keep you healthy.

Do not be envious of others. Trust me, they have their own problems.

Travel as much as you can. It will open your mind, eyes and soul.

Cooking and gardening make me happy. When you are happy, you feel better.

Good food helps you and others to be well.

Have an appetite for something in life.

Plant foods that are easy to grow...
less work.

Judge no one as we are all imperfect.

When you eat from your garden, you know what you are eating.

You can impress others, but God knows who you really are.

Be happy with yourself and like yourself.

Blaming the world is of no use. Look at yourself and the part you played.

If someone is hungry, feed them.

Do what is right for you as well as for others.

Home is always home, no matter where you are in the world.

Enjoy and love what you learn in life.
You will remember it more and be
good at it.

Help a stranger for no reason or personal gain.

Ensure your retirement. Have a house to live in and a garden to eat from.

Be healthy if you want to travel. You will enjoy your trip more.

Have a holiday at home.

A beach is a beach no matter where it is.

Every city has a harbour bridge.

Politicians are here to be of service to the people.

Those with unpaid fines should do community service.

No point fighting with others, there is enough of that in the world. Why bring it to your home?

No one should go to war for the
government.

War is a business generated by government. The little people get killed while the powers that be count their money.

Give in a way the whole community can benefit.

Feed yourself before you feed the church.

Rich people do not miss money.

Have some savings.

Money doesn't make you happy, it just makes life easier.

Your children are always on your mind as a parent. Seeing your children happy and healthy keeps you happy and healthy.

Just be happy. The rest is bullshit.

Every person should have something that is theirs. For me it was my fishing and gardening.

Something is better than nothing.

Being angry is exhausting. Its easier to flow towards what makes you happy and healthier too.

If you are nice to others, they are nice to you.

50% of nothing, is nothing…

About the Author

Christina has always had a passion for learning about health and for sharing those skills when helping others. A registered nurse with many years' experience, Christina's deep interest in and intensive study of astrology, combined with her spiritual beliefs, encouraged her journey into holistic medicine. She has gained qualifications in Ayurveda and Medical Astrology. Her book "Learn to Self-Heal" is a reflection of her experience and research into alternative healing.

Christina practises worldwide, with either Face2Face or Skype interviews, or by email. Christina lives in sunny Hawkes Bay, New Zealand, with her loving and supportive partner Andre and their awesome cat Jet. She can be contacted for her books, readings and online courses at www.christinarichterauthor.com

White Light
PUBLISHING

www.ingramcontent.com/pod-product-compliance
Lightning Source LLC
Chambersburg PA
CBHW072103290426
44110CB00014B/1803